I AM AN ELEPHANT

Aaron Carr

MEDIA ENHANCED BOOKS
AV² BY WEIGL™
ADDED VALUE • AUDIO VISUAL

Go to **www.av2books.com**, and enter this book's unique code.

BOOK CODE

H74920

AV² by Weigl brings you media enhanced books that support active learning.

AV² provides enriched content that supplements and complements this book. Weigl's AV² books strive to create inspired learning and engage young minds in a total learning experience.

Your AV² Media Enhanced books come alive with...

Audio
Listen to sections of the book read aloud.

Key Words
Study vocabulary, and complete a matching word activity.

Video
Watch informative video clips.

Quizzes
Test your knowledge.

Embedded Weblinks
Gain additional information for research.

Slide Show
View images and captions, and prepare a presentation.

Try This!
Complete activities and hands-on experiments.

... and much, much more!

Published by AV² by Weigl
350 5th Avenue, 59th Floor New York, NY 10118
Website: www.av2books.com www.weigl.com

Carr, Aaron.
Elephant / Aaron Carr.
   p. cm. -- (I am)
 ISBN 978-1-61690-753-2 (hardcover : alk. paper) -- ISBN 978-1-61690-760-0 (softcover : alk. paper)
1. Elephant--Juvenile literature. I. Title.
 QL737.P98M328 2011
 599.67--dc22

                      2010052407

Printed in the United States of America in North Mankato, Minnesota
2 3 4 5 6 7 8 9 0 16 15 14 13 12

112012
WEP081112

Project Coordinator: Aaron Carr Art Director: Terry Paulhus

Weigl acknowledges Getty Images as the primary image supplier for this title.

I AM AN ELEPHANT

In this book, I will teach you about

- myself

- my food

- my home

- my family

and much more!

I am an elephant.

4

I am the biggest animal that lives on land.

I am 260 pounds when I am born.

I use my nose
like an arm.

10

I have ears
as big as a person.

12

13

I eat 300 pounds of food every day.

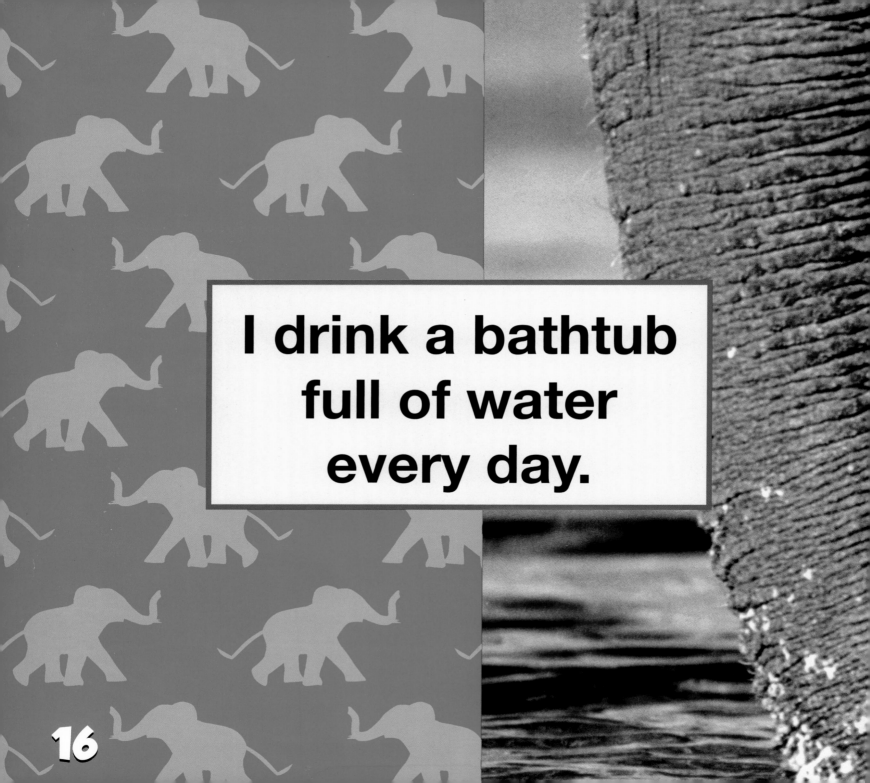

I drink a bathtub
full of water
every day.

I sleep only
three hours a day.

18

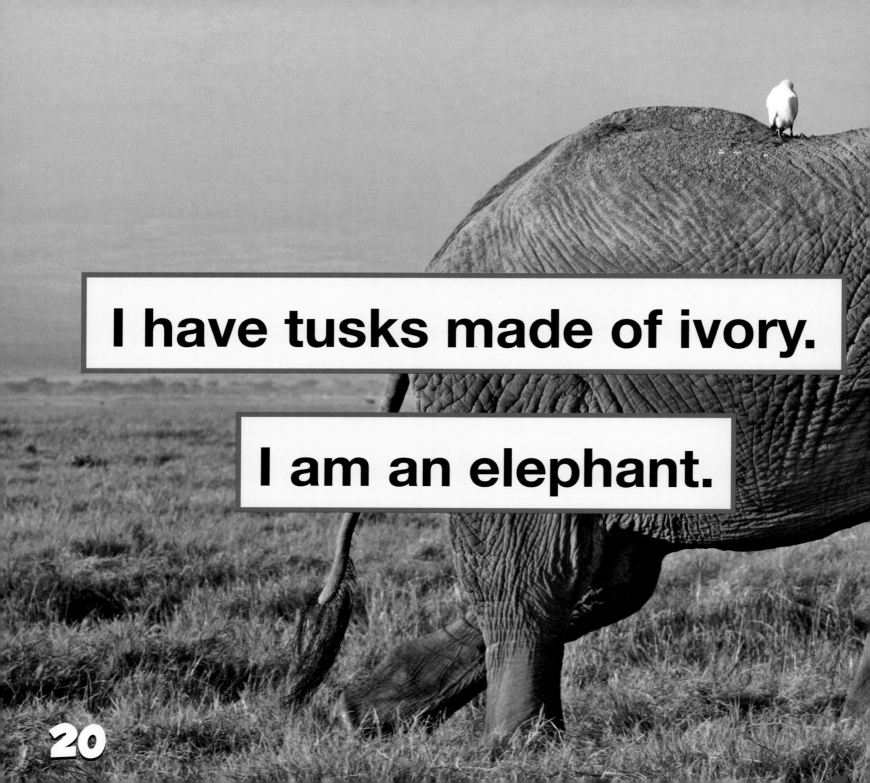

I have tusks made of ivory.

I am an elephant.

20

ELEPHANT FACTS

This page provides more detail about the interesting facts found in the book.
Simply look for the corresponding page number to match the fact.

Pages 4-5

I am an elephant. In nature, elephants live in Africa and Asia. An elephant has a huge, bulky body, and a long nose called a trunk. Two curved teeth called tusks grow on either side of the trunk. Most elephants have gray skin. This skin can be up to 1 inch (2.5 centimeters) thick.

Pages 6–7

Elephants are the biggest animals that live on land. The biggest elephant on record was 13 feet (4 meters) tall and weighed more than 25,000 pounds (11,400 kilograms). That is the size of six pick-up trucks stacked on top of each other.

Pages 8–9

Baby elephants are 260 pounds (118 kg) when they are born. This is equal to the weight of two averaged-sized people. Baby elephants are about 3 feet (91 cm) tall at birth. They are covered with fuzzy hair. A baby elephant is called a calf.

Pages 10–11

An elephant uses its nose like an arm. The trunk is used to pick up food and water, and put them in the elephant's mouth. Elephants also use their trunk to reach leaves on tall trees and to spray water on their back when they feel hot.

Pages 12–13

Elephants have ears as big as a person.
Their ears can be up to 6 feet (1.8 m) tall and 5 feet (1.5 m) wide. Elephants flap their ears back and forth to stay cool in the heat.

Pages 14–15

Elephants eat 300 pounds (136 kg) of food every day.
That is enough food to feed an average person for more than two months. An elephant's diet consists of berries, grass, leaves, tree bark, and wild fruit.

Pages 16–17

Elephants drink a bathtub full of water every day.
That is 35 gallons (132 liters) of water. It is like drinking 1,120 cans of soda. An elephant can hold as much as 3 gallons (11 L) of water in its trunk. Trunks are filled with water for many reasons. Most often, it is for drinking.

Pages 18–19

Elephants only sleep three hours a day.
Sometimes, elephants will take short rests while standing up. This type of rest is similar to when humans take a nap. Other times, elephants lie down to sleep.

Pages 20–21

Elephants have tusks made of ivory.
Ivory is used to make jewelry. Some people hunt elephants just for their tusks. The Asian elephant is now an endangered species. There are fewer than 50,000 of them in nature.

WORD LIST

Research has shown that as much as 65 percent of all written material published in English is made up of 300 words. These 300 words cannot be taught using pictures or learned by sounding them out. They must be recognized by sight. This book contains 27 common sight words to help young readers improve their reading fluency and comprehension. This book also teaches young readers several important content words, such as proper nouns. These words are paired with pictures to aid in learning and improve understanding.

Page	Sight Words	Page	Content Words
4	am, an, I	4	elephant
6	am, big, I, live, on, that, the	6	animal, land
8	am, I, when	8	born, pound
10	an, I, like, my, use	10	arm, nose
12	a, as, big, ear, have, I	12	person
14	day, eat, every, food, I, of	14	pound
16	a, day, every, full, I, of, water	16	bathtub, drink
18	a, day, I, only, sleep, three	18	hour
20	am, an, have, I, made, of	20	elephant, ivory, tusk

Check out av2books.com for activities, videos, audio clips, and more!

1 Go to av2books.com

2 Enter book code H74920

3 Explore your elephant book!

www.av2books.com